TOROSAURUS

and Other Dinosaurs of the Badlands Digs in Montana

by **Dougal Dixon**

illustrated by
Steve Weston and James Field

PICTURE WINDOW BOOKS
Minneapolis, Minnesota

Picture Window Books
151 Good Counsel Drive
P.O. Box 669
Mankato, MN 56002-0669
877-845-8392
www.picturewindowbooks.com

Printed in the United States of America.

Library of Congress Cataloging-in-Publication Data
Dixon, Dougal.
Torosaurus and other dinosaurs of the Badlands digs
in Montana / by Dougal Dixon ; illustrated by Steve
Weston and James Fields.
p. cm. — (Dinosaur find)
Includes bibliographical references and index.
ISBN-13: 978-1-4048-4716-3 (library binding)
1. Torosaurus—Juvenile literature. 2. Dinosaurs—
Montana—Juvenile literature. 3. Paleontology—
Montana—Juvenile literature. 4. Badlands—
Montana—Juvenile literature. I. Weston, Steve, ill.
II. Field, James, 1959- ill. III. Title.
QE862.O65D5955 2009
567.909786—dc22   2008006349

Acknowledgments
This book was produced for Picture Window Books
by Bender Richardson White, U.K.

Illustrations by James Field (pages 4–5, 7, 9, 15, 19)
and Steve Weston (cover and pages 11, 13, 17, 21).
Diagrams by Stefan Chabluk.

Photographs: BigStockphoto page 12 (Tiffany
Muff); Frank Lane Picture Agency pages 8 (Silvestris
Fotoservice/FLPA), 14 (R & M Van Nostrand/FLPA);
iStockphoto pages 6 (Gary Wales), 10 (Chris
Crafter), 16 (Ralf Hirsch), 18 (Roman Kazmin),
20 (Paul Benefield).

Consultant: John Stidworthy, Scientific Fellow of
the Zoological Society, London, and former
Lecturer in the Education Department, Natural
History Museum, London.

Types of dinosaurs
In this book, a red shape at the
top of a left-hand page shows
the animal was a meat-eater.
A green shape shows it was
a plant-eater.

**Just how big—or small—
were they?**
Dinosaurs were many different
sizes. We have compared their
size to one of the following:

Chicken
2 feet (60 centimeters) tall
Weight 6 pounds (2.7 kilograms)

Adult person
6 feet (1.8 meters) tall
Weight 170 pounds (76.5 kg)

Elephant
10 feet (3 m) tall
Weight 12,000 pounds
(5,400 kg)

TABLE OF CONTENTS

Life in the Badlands . . 4

Tyrannosaurus 6

Chirostenotes 8

Dromaeosaurus 10

Thescelosaurus 12

Parasaurolophus . . . 14

Dracorex 16

Edmontonia 18

Torosaurus 20

Where Did They Go? . 22

Glossary 23

To Learn More 24

Index 24

WHAT'S INSIDE?

Dinosaurs! These dinosaurs lived in what is now the Badlands area of Montana in the United States. Find out how they survived millions of years ago and what they have in common with today's animals.

Life in the Badlands

Dinosaurs lived between 230 million and 65 million years ago. The world did not look the same then. At the very end of the Age of Dinosaurs, the dry area that is now the Badlands of Montana was covered in forests. Many kinds of dinosaurs lived there.

Herds of two kinds of dinosaurs, *Parasaurolophus* and *Edmontosaurus*, gathered in an open area of a forest. A fierce *Tyrannosaurus* watched them. A little *Chirostenotes* saw the danger and escaped.

TYRANNOSAURUS

Pronunciation:
tie-RAN-uh-SAW-rus

Tyrannosaurus was the biggest meat-eating dinosaur in the Badlands forests. It hunted herds of duck-billed dinosaurs such as *Edmontosaurus*. *Tyrannosaurus* had huge, powerful jaws and teeth that could rip flesh and bone.

Big hunters today

A modern leopard is a powerful hunter on today's African plains. Once it has killed its prey, the leopard eats slowly, just like *Tyrannosaurus* once did.

Size Comparison

A *Tyrannosaurus* rushed at an *Edmontosaurus* herd. The herd scattered, but the *Tyrannosaurus* killed one of the animals and prepared to eat it.

CHIROSTENOTES

Pronunciation:
kye-ROSS-ten-OH-tees

Small meat-eaters such as *Chirostenotes* lived at the same time as the enormous *Tyrannosaurus*. *Chirostenotes* hunted for small animals and sometimes raided the nests of bigger dinosaurs.

Egg-stealers today

Modern crows are famous for wrecking the nests of other birds. They eat the other birds' eggs, just like *Chirostenotes* once did.

Size Comparison

A pair of *Chirostenotes* uncovered a fresh *Tyrannosaurus* nest. With their long-fingered hands, they picked up the eggs, broke the shells, and gobbled up the contents.

DROMAEOSAURUS

Pronunciation:
DROH-mee-uh-SAW-rus

Dromaeosaurus was one of the most active of the small meat-eating dinosaurs of the ancient Badlands. It could chase and catch really fast animals such as lizards. *Dromaeosaurus* kept warm with a covering of feathers.

Reptile hunters today

The modern secretary bird is about the same size as *Dromaeosaurus* once was. It also hunts small, fast animals.

Size Comparison

In the undergrowth, a *Dromaeosaurus* came across a lizard. The dinosaur would use its hands to catch and its teeth to kill the reptile.

THESCELOSAURUS

Pronunciation:
THES-ke-lo-SAW-rus

Thescelosaurus was a two-footed plant-eater similar in size to the modern cow. It had a beak at the front of its mouth that was used for cropping plants. In the forests, *Thescelosaurus* had to watch out for big meat-eaters such as *Tyrannosaurus*.

Sheltering animals today

Modern deer live in forests, just like *Thescelosaurus* once did. There is plenty of shelter among the trees and ferns.

Size Comparison

Thescelosaurus sheltered under the ferns of the undergrowth.

PARASAUROLOPHUS

Pronunciation:
PAR-uh-SAW-ro-LOH-fus

The strangest of the big, duck-billed dinosaurs of **65 million** years ago was *Parasaurolophus*. It had a long crest that swept back from the head. The crest was made of bony tubes. *Parasaurolophus* could blow through its crest, making honking or hooting noises.

Noisy animals today

The modern saiga antelope has a big nose. It can blow through the nose and make a loud noise, just like *Parasaurolophus* did long ago.

Size Comparison

14

A big male *Parasaurolophus* bellowed out signals to the rest of its herd. The noise helped keep the herd members safe from predators such as *Tyrannosaurus*.

DRACOREX

Pronunciation:
DRACK-oh-REX

Dracorex was one of several bone-headed dinosaurs. The bony dome was not as big as that of some other dinosaurs, but it had scary spikes. The spikes made *Dracorex* look fierce, like a dragon.

Spiky heads today

Modern ibex use their horns for showing off, just like *Dracorex* once did. Big horns might make the lead goat feel very important.

Size Comparison

Two male *Dracorex* faced one another in a power struggle. They fought for many minutes. Then, one of the males backed down, leaving the other as the winner and new leader of the herd.

EDMONTONIA

Pronunciation:
ED-mawn-TOH-nee-uh

Edmontonia was an armored dinosaur in the ancient Montana forests. Its back was covered in armor and big spikes. The spikes stuck out sideways from the shoulders and neck. They kept *Edmontonia* safe from the meat-eating *Tyrannosaurus*.

Protectors today

When threatened, modern zebras stay together so no individual is easy to catch. Long ago, *Edmontonia* would have done the same.

Size Comparison

Edmontonia bunched together so an attacking *Tyrannosaurus* could not get past the defensive rows of spikes.

TOROSAURUS

Pronunciation:
TOR-uh-SAW-rus

Torosaurus had the biggest head of all of the dinosaurs. *Torosaurus* was a horned dinosaur with a very long shield protecting its neck and shoulders. It also had three horns on its face—a pair above the eyes and one on the nose.

Declining animals today

Torosaurus was one of the last dinosaurs. Today, whales are not as common as they used to be. Some people fear they will become extinct some day, just like *Torosaurus* once did.

Size Comparison

With its narrow beak, *Torosaurus* nipped off the tasty twigs in the forests at the very end of the Age of Dinosaurs.

WHERE DID THEY GO?

Dinosaurs are extinct, which means that none of them are alive today. Scientists study rocks and fossils to find clues about what happened to dinosaurs.

People have different explanations about what happened. Some people think a huge asteroid that hit Earth caused all sorts of climate changes, which caused the dinosaurs to die. Others think volcanic eruptions caused the climate change and that killed the dinosaurs. No one knows for sure what happened to all of the dinosaurs.

GLOSSARY

beak—the hard front part of the mouth of birds and some dinosaurs; also called a bill

crest—a structure on top of the head, usually used to signal to other animals

duck-billed—to have a broad, flat beak, or bill, like that of a duck

ferns—plants with finely divided leaves known as fronds; ferns are common in damp woods and on mountains

herd—a large group of animals that move, feed, and sleep together

prey—an animal that is hunted and eaten for food

reptile—a cold-blooded animal with a backbone and scales; it walks on short legs or crawls on its belly

signal—to make a sign, warning, or hint

To Learn More

More Books to Read

Clark, Neil, and William Lindsay. *1001 Facts About Dinosaurs.* New York: Dorling Kindersley, 2002.

Dixon, Dougal. *Dougal Dixon's Amazing Dinosaurs.* Honesdale, Penn.: Boyds Mills Press, 2007.

Holtz, Thomas R., and Michael Brett-Surman. *Jurassic Park Institute Dinosaur Field Guide.* New York: Random House, 2001.

On the Web

FactHound offers a safe, fun way to find Web sites related to topics in this book. All of the sites on FactHound have been researched by our staff.

1. Visit *www.facthound.com*

2. Type in this special code: 1404847162

3. Click on the FETCH IT button.

Your trusty FactHound will fetch the best Web sites for you!

Index

armored, 18

beak, 12, 21

bone-headed, 16

Chirostenotes, 5, 8–9

crest, 14

Dracorex, 16–17

Dromaeosaurus, 10–11

duck-bills, 6, 14

Edmontonia, 18–19

Edmontosaurus, 5, 6, 7

eggs, 8, 9

feathers, 10

herds, 5, 6, 7, 15, 17

horns, 16, 20

meat-eaters, 6, 8, 10, 12, 18

noises, 14, 15

Parasaurolophus, 5, 14–15

plant-eaters, 12

teeth, 6, 11

Thescelosaurus, 12–13

Torosaurus, 20–21

Tyrannosaurus, 5, 6–7, 8, 9, 12, 15, 18, 19

Look for other books in the Dinosaur Find series: